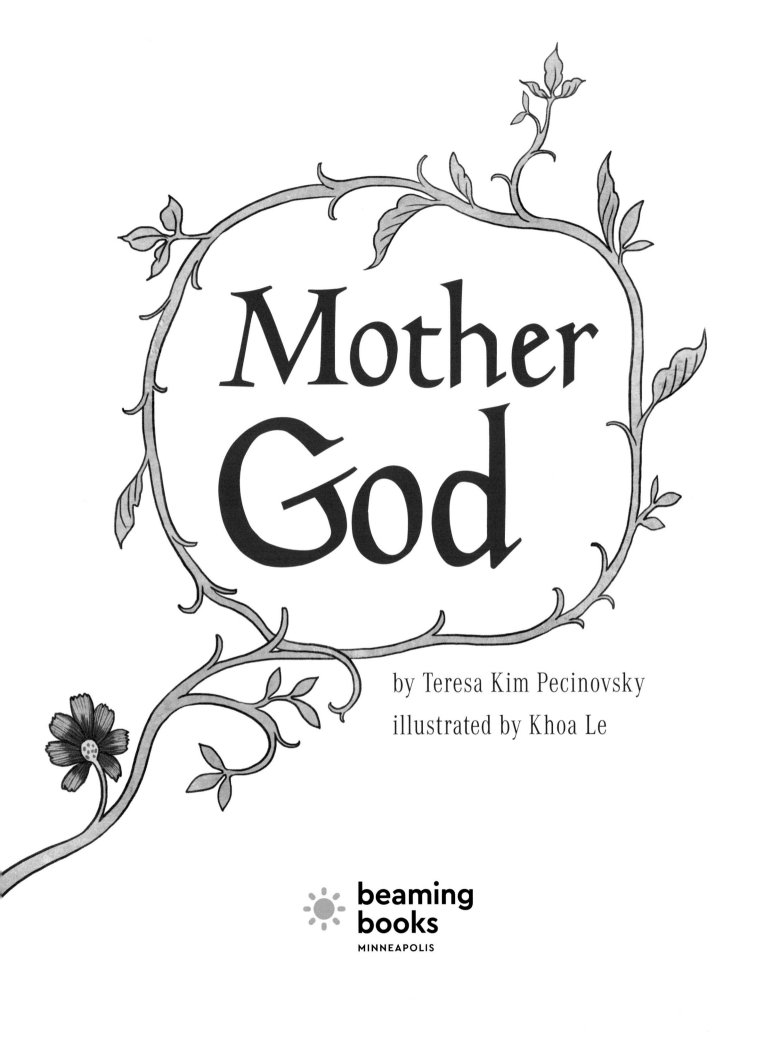

Mother God

by Teresa Kim Pecinovsky

illustrated by Khoa Le

beaming books

MINNEAPOLIS

You know God the Father,
But God is your Mother too.
You are made in Her image—
She is making all things new.

Waiting for new life to begin,
God is a mother in labor.

She takes deep breaths until the birth,
Rejoicing with friend and neighbor.

Throughout day and night, God wakes
To nurse the infant at Her side.
She snuggles Her baby gently
Until he closes his sleepy eyes.

When baby tumbles on the floor,
God pulls off each tiny sock.

She holds Her arms out wide
And the baby learns to walk.

God is Sophia Wisdom,
Teaching what is true and right.

Wisdom works, creates, orders, and plays.
She calls us with joy and delight.

Over the waters of creation,
God is the Spirit who hovers.
She forms the Earth into a bed,
And the wide sky, its covers.

God is a Mother hen
Who gathers chicks under Her wings.
She plays hide-and-seek in soft grass,
Behind trees, and quiet springs.

She protects Her cubs from danger,
God, the great Mother Bear.
As fierce as She is tender,
She guards them in Her care.

God is a lurking leopard,

Secretive, skilled, and strong.

Teaching Her young to swim and climb,

She roars and they tag along.

With a huge supply of flour
God kneads and bakes good bread.
She feeds Her entire neighborhood;
They feast and all are fed.

God is a skillful seamstress
Who stitches and sews thread together.
She makes clothes for rain, snow, and sun,
Caring for you in all kinds of weather.

Granny, Baba, Halmeoni,
God is a woman with gray hair.
She passes down stories of old,
Rocking softly in a chair.

She is the God who sees you.

God weeps, mourns, and cries.

She comforts you through the longest night,

Keeping watch until sunrise.

She quiets us with Her songs,
Singing lullabies in the night.
God, our nurturing Mother,
Wraps us in holy moonlight.

God is your loving Mother—
You are made in Her image too.
God calls you "Beloved."
She is making all things new.

For 선아 and 서희
—TKP

To my mother
—KL

Published in 2022 by Beaming Books, an imprint of 1517 Media. All rights reserved.
No part of this book may be reproduced without the written permission of the publisher.
Email copyright@1517.media. Printed in the United States of America.

28 27 26 25 24 23 22   4 5 6 7 8 9

Hardcover ISBN: 978-1-5064-7901-9
eBook ISBN: 978-1-5064-8171-5

Library of Congress Cataloging-in-Publication Data
Names: Pecinovsky, Teresa Kim, author. | Le, Khoa, illustrator.
Title: Mother God / by Teresa Kim Pecinovsky ; illustrated by Khoa Le.
Description: Minneapolis, MN : Beaming Books, 2022. | Audience: Ages 3-8 |
    Summary: "Mother God introduces readers to a dozen images of God
    inspired by feminine descriptions from Scripture"-- Provided by
    publisher.
Identifiers: LCCN 2021028792 (print) | LCCN 2021028793 (ebook) | ISBN
    9781506479019 (hardcover) | ISBN 9781506481715 (ebook)
Subjects: LCSH: God--Juvenile literature. | Femininity of God--Juvenile
    literature.
Classification: LCC BT107 .P395 2022 (print) | LCC BT107 (ebook) | DDC
    231--dc23
LC record available at https://lccn.loc.gov/2021028792
LC ebook record available at https://lccn.loc.gov/2021028793

VN0006065; 9781506479019; FEB2022

Beaming Books
PO Box 1209
Minneapolis, MN 55440-1209
Beamingbooks.com